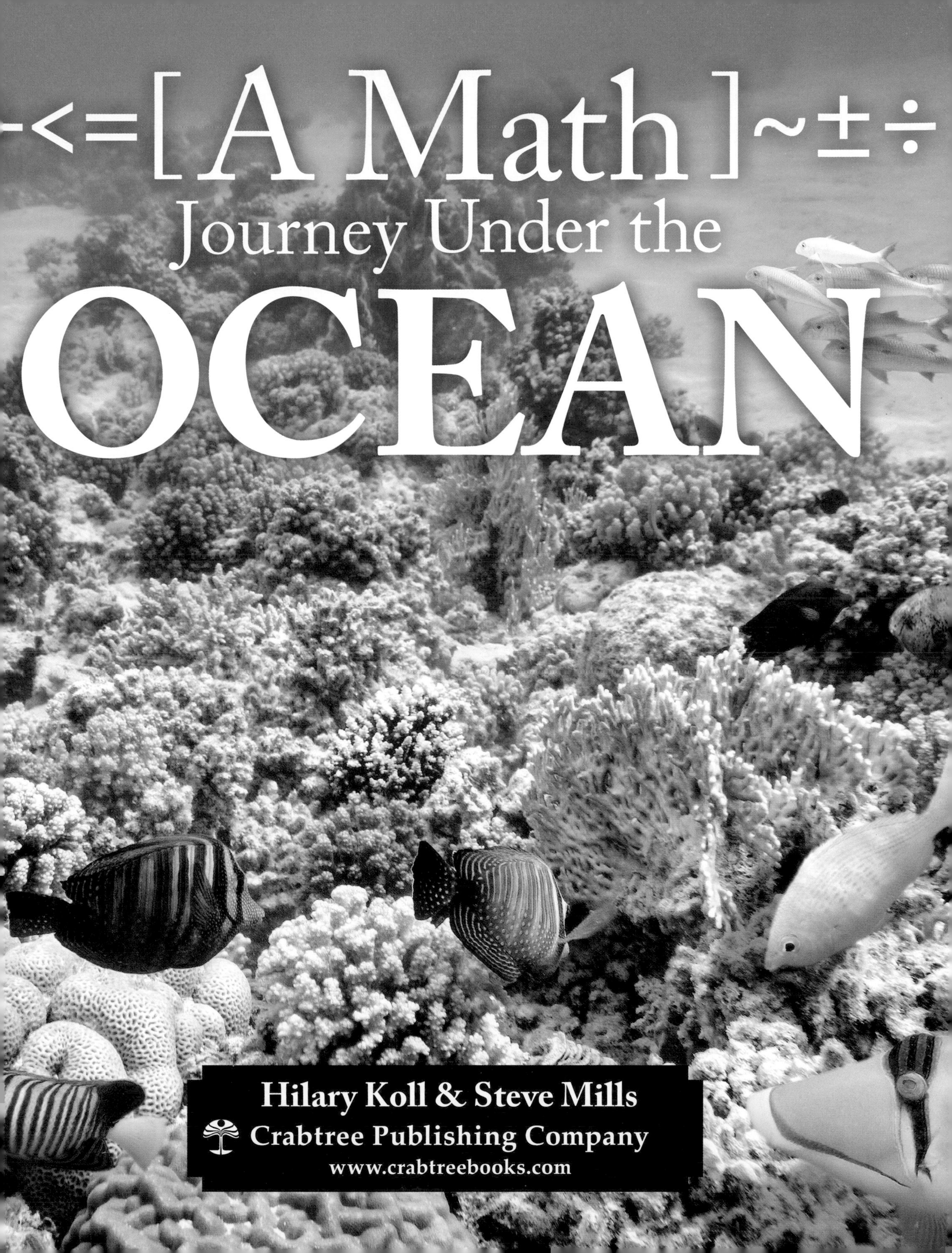

-<=[A Math]~±÷
Journey Under the
OCEAN

Hilary Koll & Steve Mills

Crabtree Publishing Company
www.crabtreebooks.com

Crabtree Publishing Company
www.crabtreebooks.com
1-800-387-7650

Published in Canada
616 Welland Ave.
St. Catharines, ON
L2M 5V6

Published in the United States
PMB 59051, 350 Fifth Ave.
59th Floor,
New York, NY

Published in 2016 by CRABTREE PUBLISHING COMPANY.

First published in 2016 by Wayland
(A division of Hachette Children's Books)

Author: Hilary Koll and Steve Mills
Commissioning editor: Elizabeth Brent
Content Review: Diane Dakers
Editors: Joe Fullman, Rob Colson and Kathy Middleton
Proofreader: Janine Deschenes
Math Consultant: Diane Dakers
Designer: Ed Simkins
Prepress technician: Katherine Berti
Print and production coordinator: Katherine Berti

Production coordinated by Tall Tree Ltd

Photographs:
Istockphoto: 4-5 strmko, 6–7 VitalyEdush, 14–15 Snaprender, 22–23 Tenedos, 26-27 richcarey
All other images by Shutterstock.

Printed in Canada/022016/IH20151223

Library and Archives Canada Cataloguing in Publication

Koll, Hilary, author
A math journey under the ocean / Hilary Koll, Steve Mills.

(Go figure!)
Includes index.
Issued in print and electronic formats.
ISBN 978-0-7787-2315-8 (bound).--
ISBN 978-0-7787-2327-1 (paperback).--
ISBN 978-1-4271-7718-6 (html)

1. Mathematics--Juvenile literature. 2. Ocean--Juvenile literature.
I. Mills, Steve, author II. Title.

QA40.5.K658 2016 j510 C2015-907939-X
C2015-907940-3

Library of Congress Cataloging-in-Publication Data

Names: Koll, Hilary, author. | Mills, Steve, 1955- author.
Title: A math journey under the ocean / Hilary Koll and Steve Mills.
Description: New York, New York : Crabtree Publishing Company, 2016. | Series: Go figure! | Includes index.
Identifiers: LCCN 2015049847 (print) | LCCN 2016000173 (ebook)
ISBN 9780778723158 (reinforced library binding : alk. paper)
ISBN 9780778723271 (pbk. : alk. paper)
ISBN 9781427177186 (electronic HTML)
Subjects: LCSH: Oceanography--Mathematics--Juvenile literature. | Ocean--Juvenile literature. | Mathematics--Juvenile literature.
Classification: LCC GC10.4.M36 K65 2016 (print) | LCC GC10.4.M36 (ebook) | DDC 551.46--dc23
LC record available at http://lccn.loc.gov/2015049847

go figure! Stand by to plunge beneath the waves! Use your mathematical skills to study and explore the ocean depths.

CONTENTS

Words in **bold** appear in the glossary on pages 30–31.

Answers to the Go Figure! challenges can be found on page 28.

Please note: The imperial and metric systems are used interchangeably throughout this book.

WHAT EQUIPMENT DO YOU NEED?

Pen or pencil

Notepad

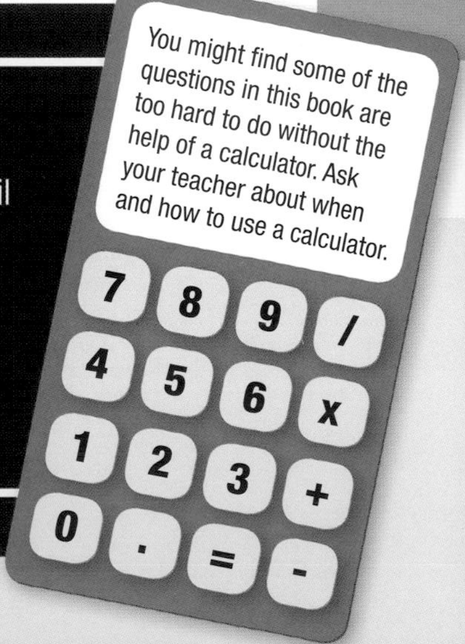
You might find some of the questions in this book are too hard to do without the help of a calculator. Ask your teacher about when and how to use a calculator.
7 8 9 /
4 5 6 x
1 2 3 +
0 . = -

MISSION 1

LEARNING TO DIVE

Your first mission is to make sure you are ready to dive, so you can explore the underwater world safely.

LEARN ABOUT IT NEGATIVE NUMBERS

Negative numbers are numbers that are less than zero. Positive numbers are numbers that are greater than zero.

The surface of an ocean is called sea level. To measure how high a mountain is or how deep something is under the ocean, we start our measurement from sea level. If sea level is at zero, then each meter below sea level can be described as a negative number. One meter below sea level is written as -1, two meters below is -2, and so on.

You know that the number 20 is lower than 30, but it works the opposite way for negative numbers. The number -20 is actually higher than -30. See for yourself on the number line shown to the right.

When diving or rising from an underwater position, count up or down the number line. For example, if you are at -20 m and dive five meters lower, count downward from -20 to -25.

To find how far two negative numbers are apart on a number line, you can count the interval, or the distance, between the two numbers. The interval will be the same as if the numbers were both positive. For example, this number line shows that the distance between -30 and -5 is 25. It is the same as the distance between 30 and 5.

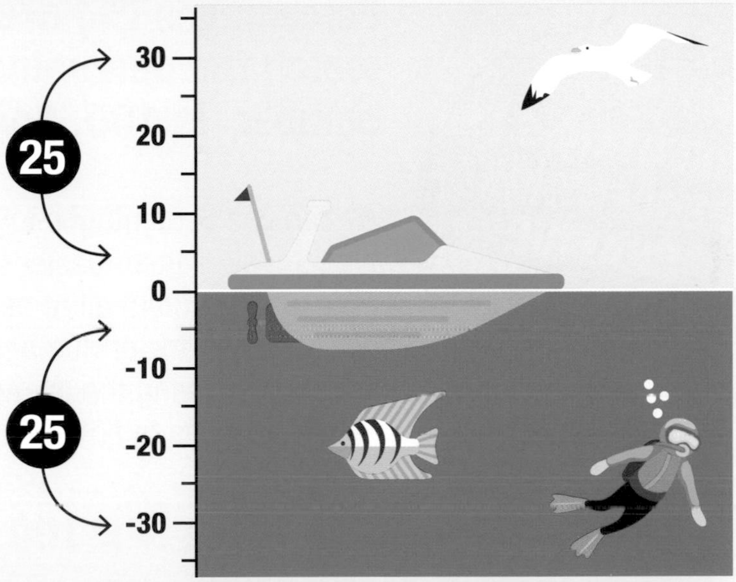

›GO FIGURE!

It's important to know how far below the surface you are when diving. Going too deep can make you sick. For your own safety, answer these questions using the number lines on these pages to help count:

1. Here are some depths below sea level: -6 m, -32 m, -18 m, -40 m, -25 m
   a) Which of these is the deepest? b) Put them in order, from highest to deepest.

2. You dive down to a depth of -35 m (35 meters below sea level).
   a) If you rise by 10 m, what depth would you be at? b) From this new position, what depth would you be at if you dove down a further 17 m?

3. You are at -28 m. If you want to get to -7 m, how many meters must you rise?

4. An octopus is at -31 m. How many meters is the octopus below you if you are at: a) -3 m, b) -16 m, c) 2 m above sea level, inside the boat?

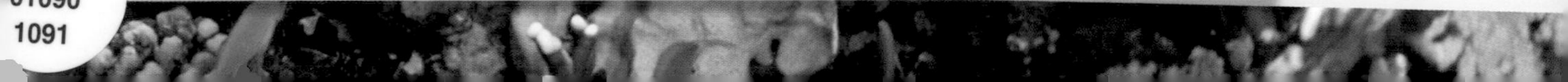

CORAL REEFS

Your next mission takes you to the world's coral reefs. Home to many colorful plants and animals, these underwater ecosystems are being threatened by human activities. Measure the reefs and note any changes.

LEARN ABOUT IT: PERCENTAGES AND PERCENTAGE CHANGE

Percentages **(%) are fractions in which the denominator, or bottom number, is 100. For example, 75% =** $\frac{75}{100}$

We can use percentages to describe fractions in a way that makes them easier to compare. To compare fractions, change them all to percentages by dividing the fraction's numerator, or number on the top, by its denominator, and then multiplying the answer by 100. The example below compares three fractions to find out which one is the largest.

$\frac{3}{4}$ **as a percentage is** $3 \div 4 \times 100 = 75\%$

$\frac{160}{250}$ **is** $160 \div 250 \times 100 = 64\%$

$\frac{63}{90}$ **is** $63 \div 90 \times 100 = 70\%$

We can easily see that 75% is greater than 70% and 64%, so ¾ is the largest of the three fractions.

To compare how much things have changed over time, find the percentage it increased or decreased by, like this:

$$\frac{\textbf{(New amount minus the original amount)}}{\textbf{Original amount}} \times 100$$

For example, if a piece of coral was 10 cm in length, and it grew to 12 cm over a period of time, the percentage increase is:

$$\frac{12 - 10}{10} \times 100 = 2 \div 10 \times 100 = 20\% \text{ increase}$$

>GO FIGURE!

You visit three of the world's largest coral, or barrier, reefs—the Great Barrier Reef in Australia, the Mesoamerican Barrier Reef, which runs through Mexico and Central America, and the Andros Barrier Reef in the Bahamas. You collect **data** on how much **area**, in km^2, each coral reef covers today in order to compare it with their measurements in 1999. Show the figures as percentage increases or decreases.

A) GREAT BARRIER REEF

1999	Today
250 km^2	200 km^2

B) MESOAMERICAN REEF

1999	Today
320 km^2	224 km^2

C) ANDROS BARRIER REEF

1999	Today
900 km^2	495 km^2

1. What is the difference in area, in km^2, between 1999 and the present day for: a) Reef A, b) Reef B, c) Reef C?
2. Has each reef increased or decreased in area between 1999 and the present day?
3. Find the percentage decrease for each reef using the **formula** on the previous page.
4. Which reef's area has had the greatest percentage change?
5. There used to be around 400,000 km^2 of coral reef on Earth, but there is now only about 280,000 km^2. By what percentage has the total amount of coral reef decreased?

MISSION 3

SHIPWRECK

Your next adventure is in South Africa exploring the "graveyard of ships" at the stormy Cape of Good Hope. Learn how to chart items you find using **coordinates**, or sets of numbers that identify locations on a grid.

LEARN ABOUT IT
FOUR-QUADRANT COORDINATES

The grid is divided by two lines called the x-axis (horizontal) and the y-axis (vertical). They divide the grid into four areas called quadrants**. The origin is where the x-axis meets the y-axis.**

Any point on the grid can be referred to by its coordinates. All coordinates are measured starting from the origin.

Coordinates are written as two numbers inside brackets, separated by a comma. The first number shows you the distance you have to go to the left or right across the x-axis to get to a location. The second number shows the distance you have to go up or down on the y-axis.

The point (x, y) on the grid shown here is at (3,4). This means you go 3 squares to the right from the origin, and 4 squares up to reach the point.

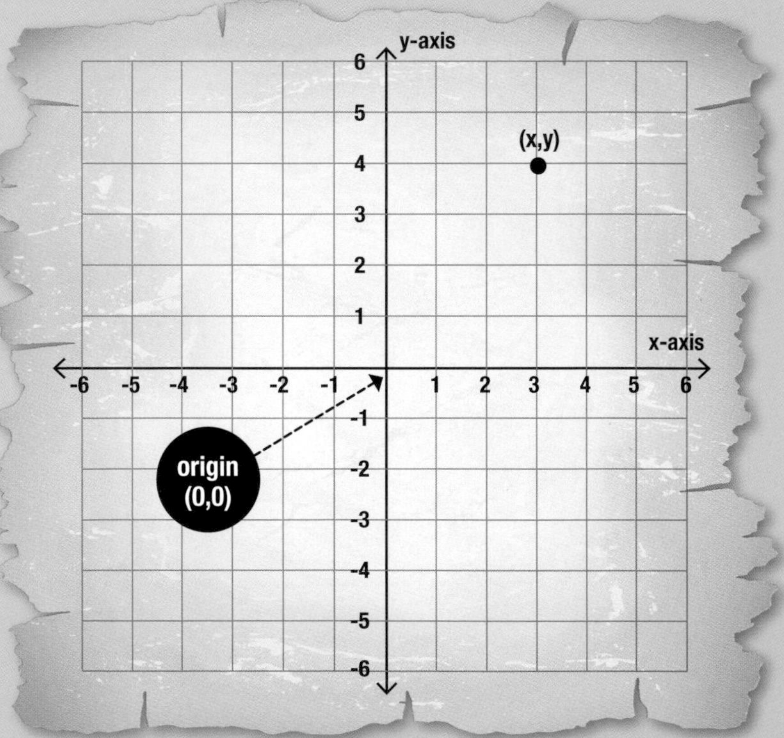

- All points on the right of the y-axis have positive x values.
- All points on the left of the y-axis have negative x values.
- All points above the x-axis have positive y values.
- All points below the x-axis have negative y values.

GO FIGURE!

You must locate the items you found around this shipwreck and collect data about their positions.

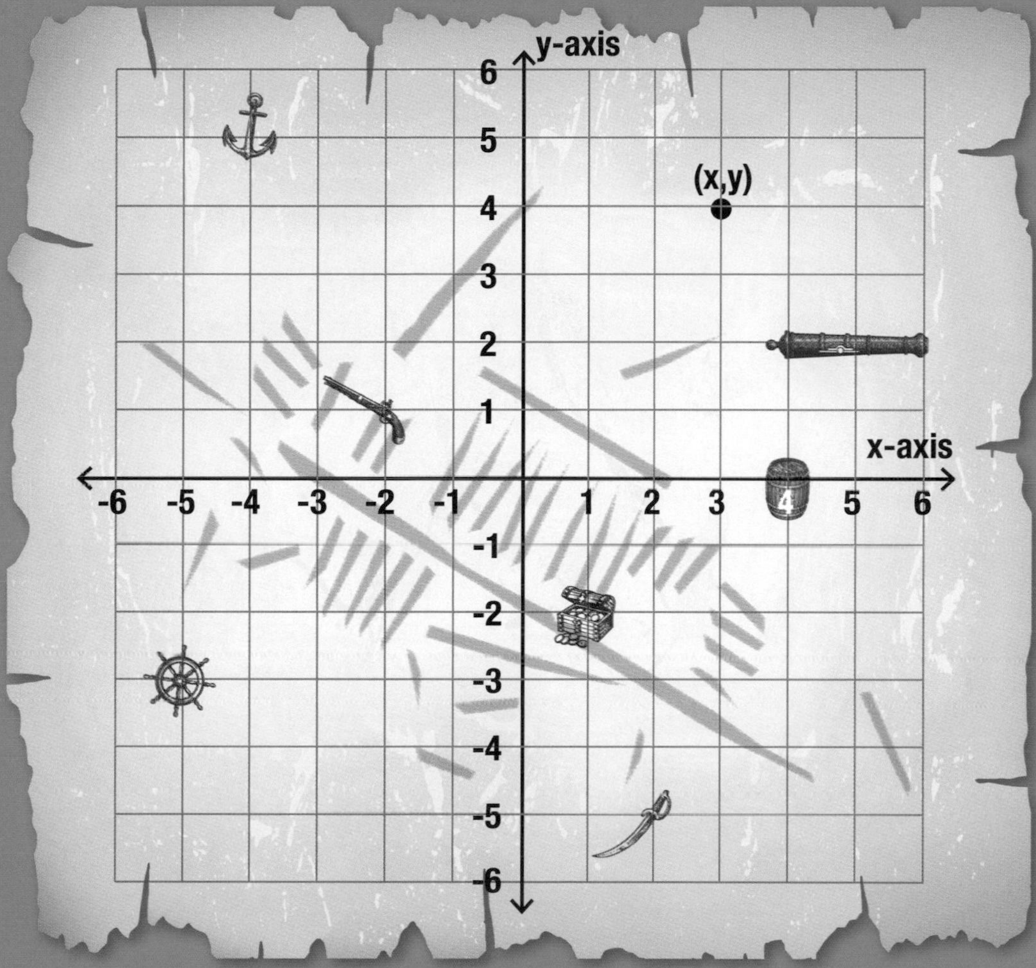

1. Chart the location where you found each item by writing their coordinates. Write the coordinates for the:
   a) anchor, b) ship's wheel,
   c) cutlass (sword), d) barrel.

2. Describe what item is located at:
   a) (1,-2), b) (-2,1).

3. The cannon lies across three points on the coordinate grid. Write all three points.

4. On your dive you have reached the point marked (x,y). How many squares and in which direction on each of the x and y axes must you move to reach the ship's wheel?

5. From (x,y) describe what you reach if you move:
   a) left 2 squares and down 6 squares,
   b) right 1 square and down 2 squares.

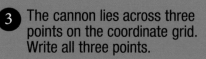

OCEAN BED

While you are down at the bottom of the sea exploring shipwrecks, use your **sonar** equipment to measure the depth of the ocean in different places. Sonar is a technology that sends out pulses of sound underwater and measures distance by recording when the echo returns.

LEARN ABOUT IT
GRAPHS AND AVERAGES

To read a bar-line graph, it's important to know what each interval, or space between lines, on the scale is worth.

Each interval on the y-axis can be figured out by dividing the first number up from zero labeled on the axis by the number of lines between that number and zero. For example, on the graph on the opposite page, 1000 divided by 5 lines means each unnumbered line is worth 200. To read the measurement of depth on the graph, follow the bar for a particular recording down to the horizontal line where the bar ends, then follow the horizontal line to the y-axis and read the depth.

The **mean average** gives us a number to represent a set of numbers. An average is useful because it gives us a number that is more representative of the whole set than the highest or lowest numbers in the set would be. To calculate the mean average of a set of numbers, add them all together, and then divide by how many numbers there are in the set.

For example, the mean average of the numbers 4, 7, 2, 9, and 8 is found by first adding them together:

$$4 + 7 + 2 + 9 + 8 = 30$$

and then dividing by how many numbers there are in the set, which is 5:

$$30 \div 5 = 6$$

The mean average of this set of numbers is 6.

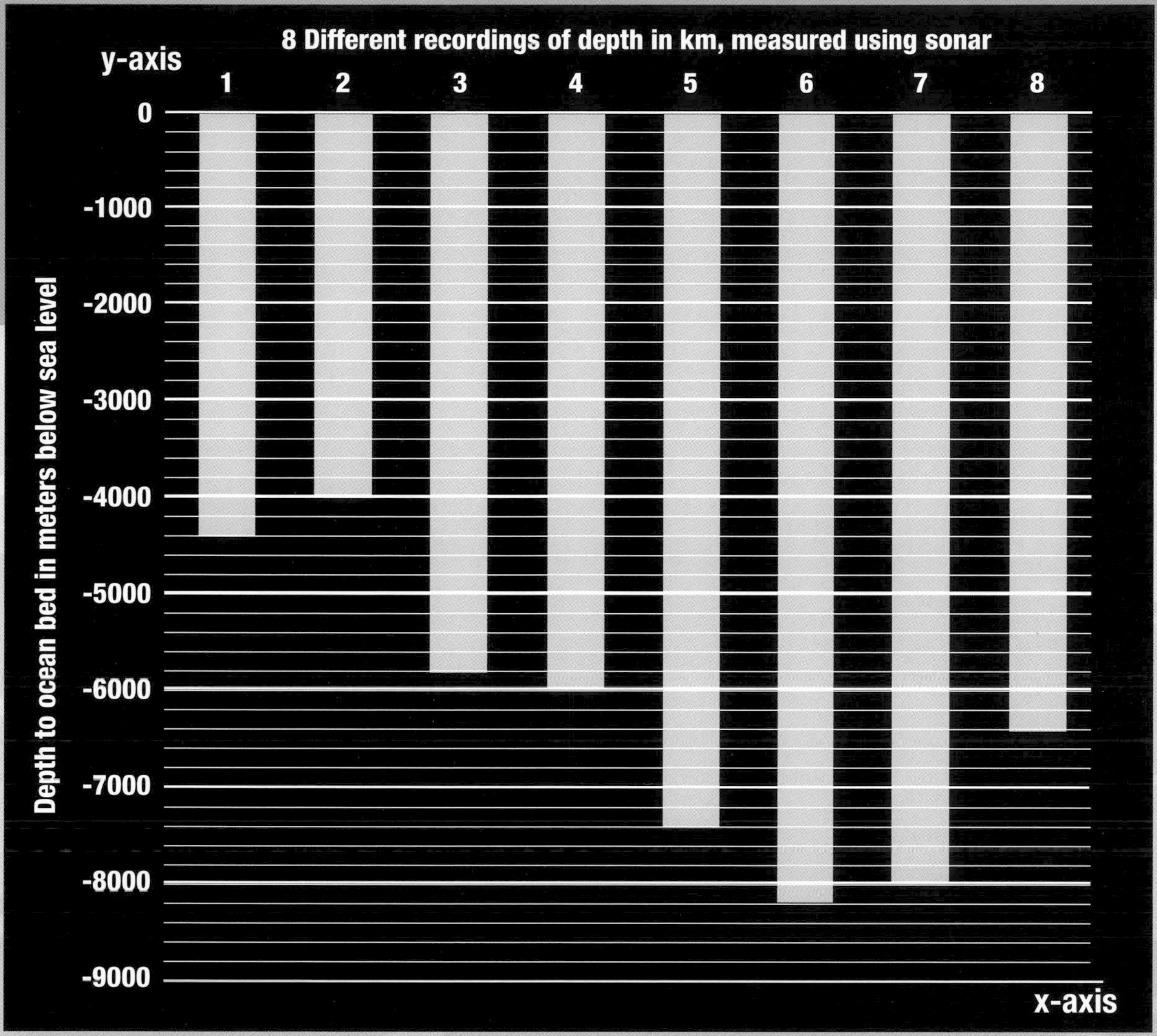

GO FIGURE!

You have taken sonar readings at eight different points, each 1 km apart. Your readings of the depth of the ocean bed are shown on the bar-line graph above.

1. Make a list of the depth of the ocean for each of the eight sonar readings.
2. How much deeper is the ocean at:
   a) point 6 than point 2,
   b) point 7 than point 4?
3. Find the mean average for the eight readings.
4. Which sonar reading is closest to this mean average and therefore the most representative of the set?

MISSION 5

SUBMARINES

You will need a submarine for your next mission to the deepest part of all the oceans. The Mariana Trench is a deep valley carved into the floor of the western part of the Pacific Ocean. First, you must learn how to figure out underwater speed and how to read your submarine's gages.

LEARN ABOUT IT
READING GAGES AND CALCULATING SPEED

When reading scales or gages, count the number of intervals between two numbers marked on the scale. To find how much each interval is worth, divide the difference between the two numbers by the number of intervals.

A **knot** is the unit of speed commonly used in maritime navigation. It is a speed of one **nautical** mile per hour.

The gage on the left measures speed in knots. It shows 10 intervals between the marks numbered 0 and 20. To figure out the **value** of each interval, first find the difference: 20 – 0 = 20. Then divide the answer by the number of intervals: 20 ÷ 10 = 2. Each interval is worth 2 knots. Here, example A is at the two interval mark, so the speed the submarine is traveling is 2 × 2 = 4 knots. Example B is at 8 intervals. Its speed is 2 × 8 = 16 knots.

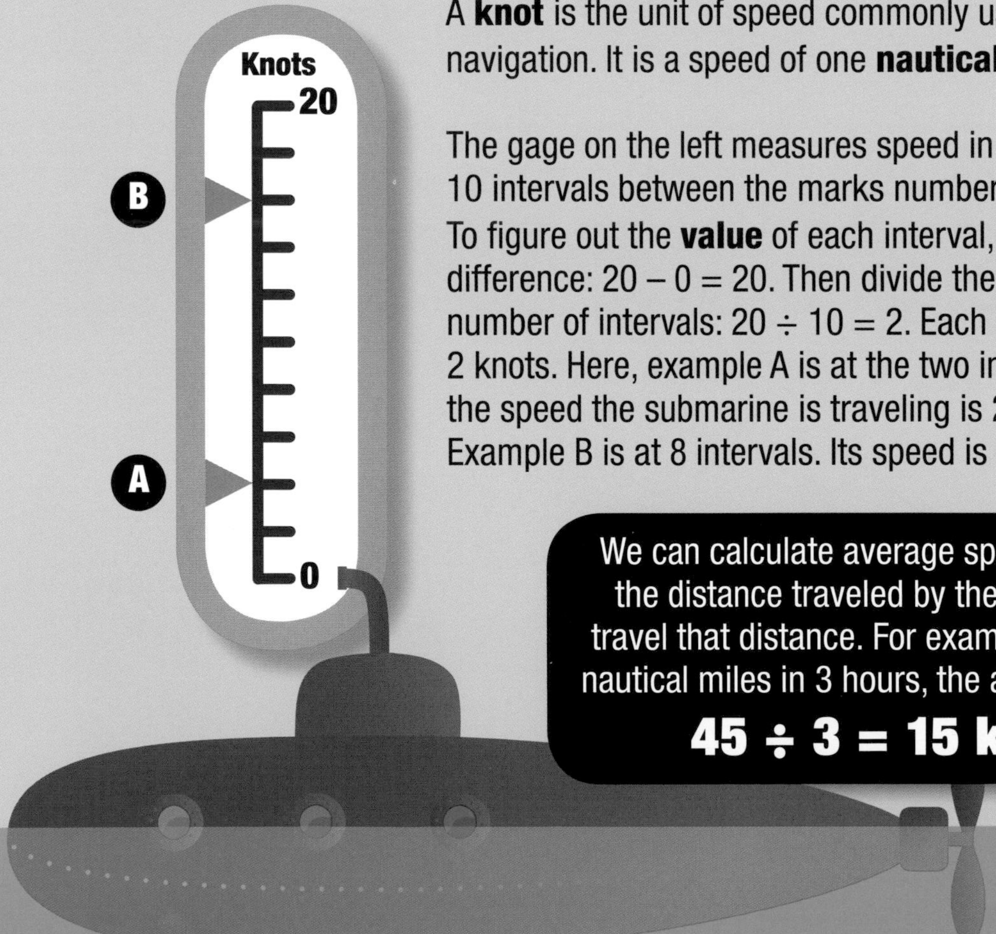

We can calculate average speed by dividing the distance traveled by the time taken to travel that distance. For example, if we go 45 nautical miles in 3 hours, the average speed is

45 ÷ 3 = 15 knots

Speeds can also be given in other units, such as miles per hour or kilometers per hour. It must match the unit the distance is given in:

If we travel 136 miles in 8 hours, the average speed is

136 ÷ 8 = 17 miles per hour (17 mph)

›GO FIGURE!

As the submarine's pilot, you must take readings from the gages in the submarine's control room.

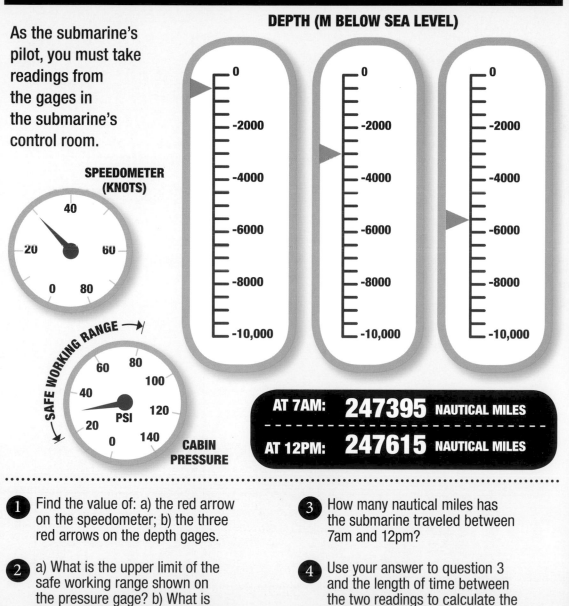

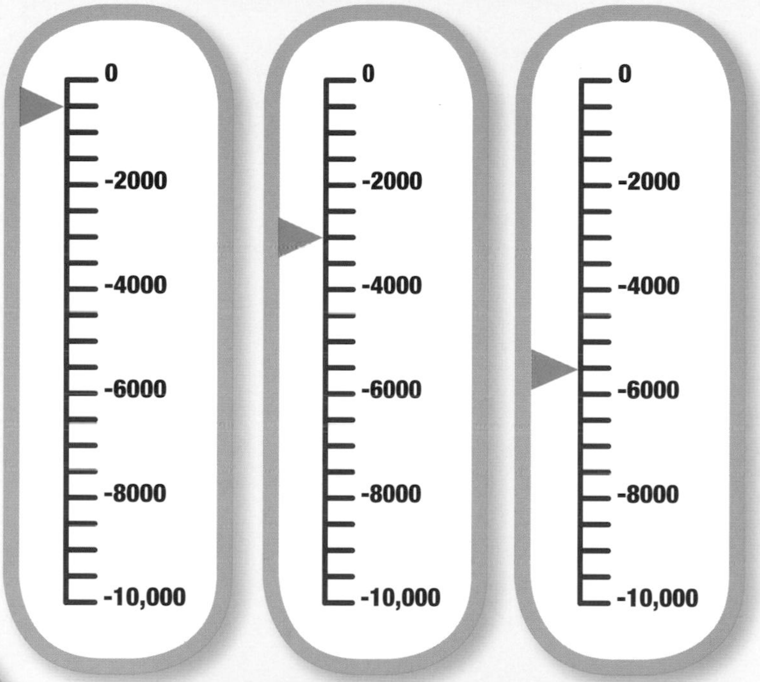

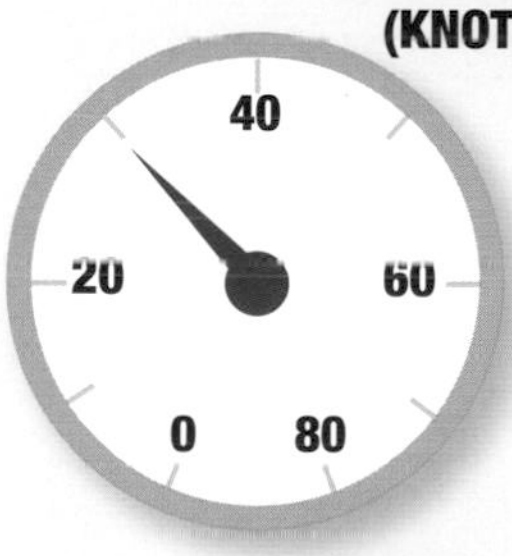

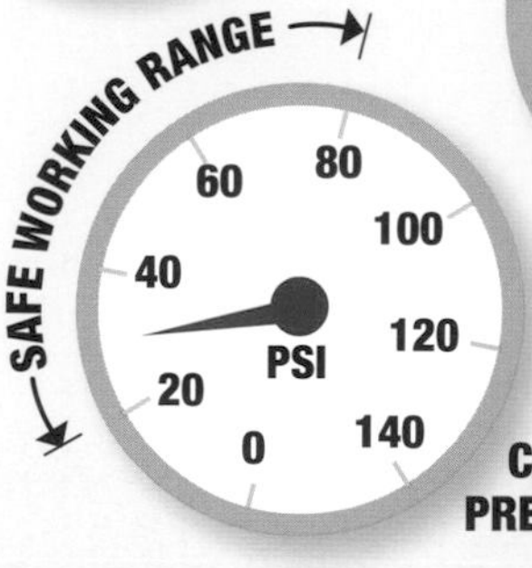

AT 7AM: **247395** NAUTICAL MILES

AT 12PM: **247615** NAUTICAL MILES

1. Find the value of: a) the red arrow on the speedometer; b) the three red arrows on the depth gages.
2. a) What is the upper limit of the safe working range shown on the pressure gage? b) What is the pressure shown by the arrow?
3. How many nautical miles has the submarine traveled between 7am and 12pm?
4. Use your answer to question 3 and the length of time between the two readings to calculate the average speed in knots.

WATCH OUT!

It is surprisingly busy under the ocean. You must avoid running into things, such as other submarines. Learn how to plot a route that avoids potential dangers.

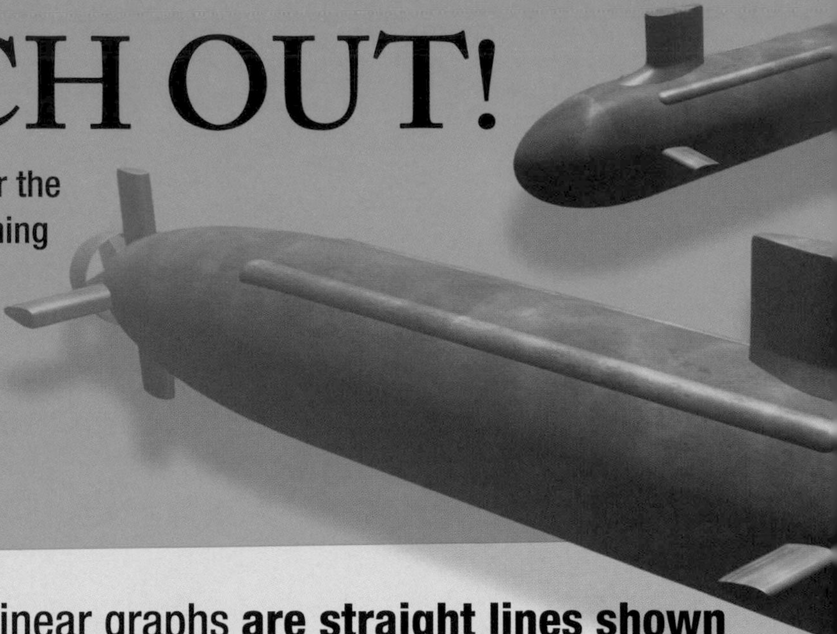

LEARN ABOUT IT
LINEAR GRAPHS

Linear graphs are straight lines shown on a coordinate grid. The coordinates of each point along the straight line share something in common.

Look at the line on this grid. Here are some coordinates of points along it: (-5,-4) (-2,-1) (-1,0) (1,2) (3,4) (5,6)

Can you see a pattern in the coordinates? The coordinate along the y-axis is always 1 more than the coordinate on the x-axis.

We can describe this particular line using the **equation**

y = x + 1

because every point along its length follows this rule.

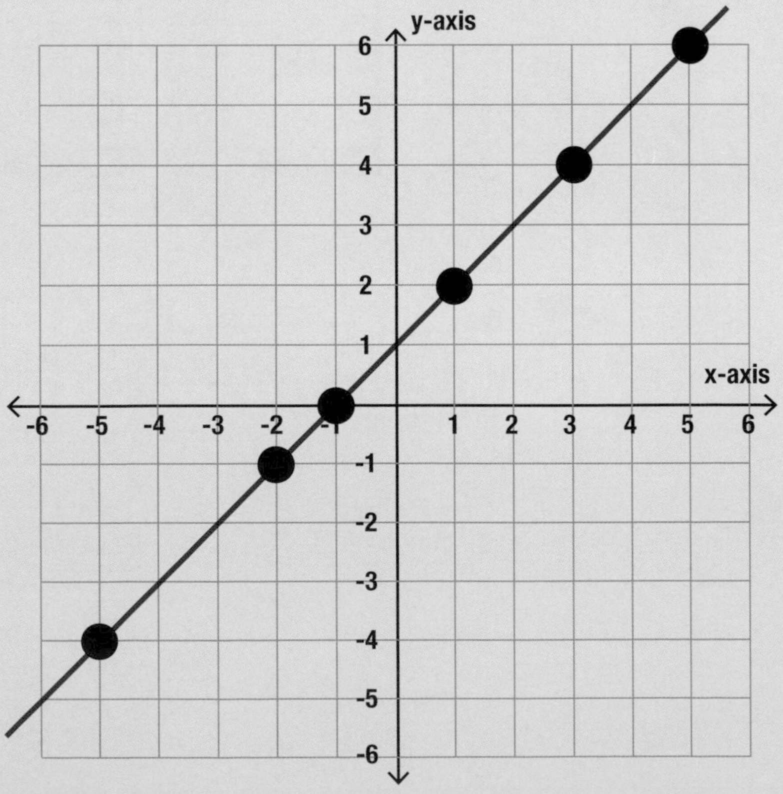

We can also figure out whether other coordinates will fall on a line. For example, (6,3) is not on the line $y = x + 1$ since the y-coordinate is not one more than the x-coordinate. We could also replace the value of x in the equation since we know it is 6. The equation becomes $y = 6 + 1$. The answer, $y = 7$, does not match the y-coordinate given, which is 3. It is not on the line.

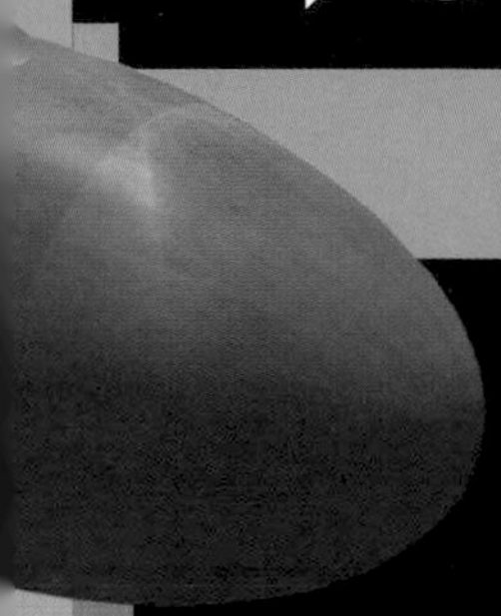

›GO FIGURE!

There is another submarine heading your way. Is your sub in its path?

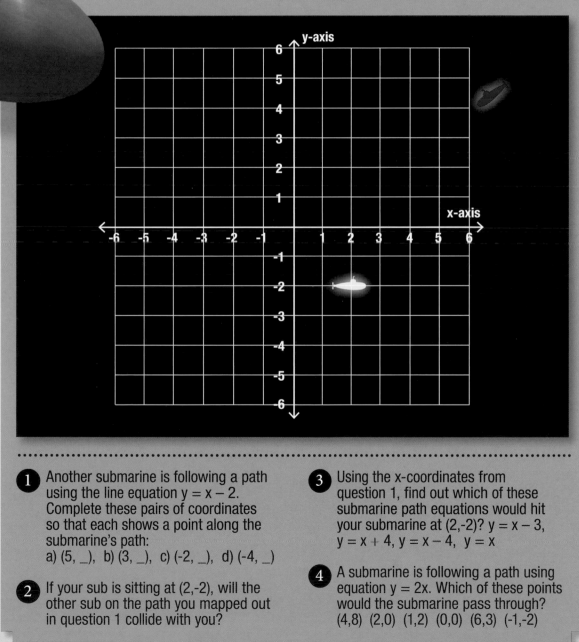

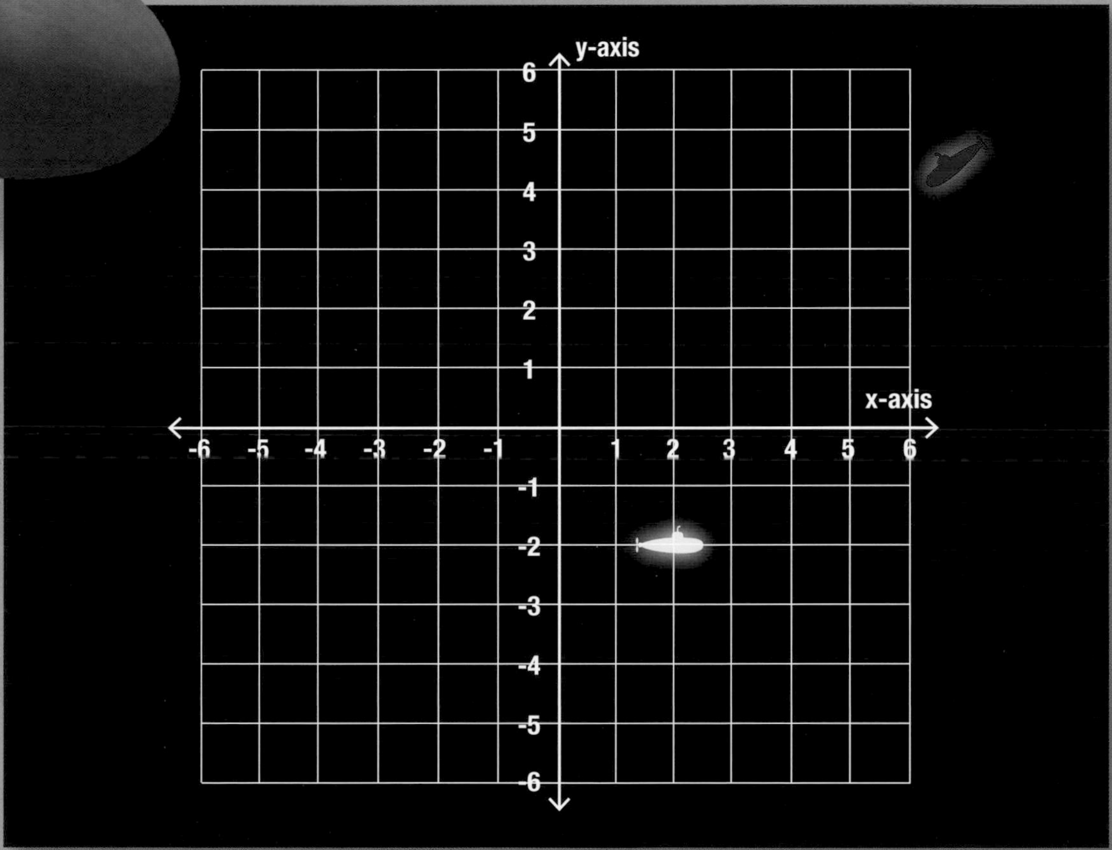

1. Another submarine is following a path using the line equation $y = x - 2$. Complete these pairs of coordinates so that each shows a point along the submarine's path:
a) (5, _), b) (3, _), c) (-2, _), d) (-4, _)

2. If your sub is sitting at (2,-2), will the other sub on the path you mapped out in question 1 collide with you?

3. Using the x-coordinates from question 1, find out which of these submarine path equations would hit your submarine at (2,-2)? $y = x - 3$, $y = x + 4$, $y = x - 4$, $y = x$

4. A submarine is following a path using equation $y = 2x$. Which of these points would the submarine pass through?
(4,8) (2,0) (1,2) (0,0) (6,3) (-1,-2)

MISSION 7

SHOALS AND SHARKS

From May to July, huge groups, or shoals, of sardines swim along the coast of South Africa. They are easy targets for hungry sharks. On this mission, figure out how much of each shoal is eaten by sharks.

LEARN ABOUT IT
PROPORTIONS AS FRACTIONS AND DECIMALS

A proportion **compares part of something with its whole. For example, someone might score 7 correct answers (part) out of 10 questions (whole) on a test.**

We can write this proportion as a fraction, $\frac{7}{10}$, or in decimal form as **0.7**. Similarly, scoring 19 out of 100 is the fraction $\frac{19}{100}$, and **0.19** is the decimal form.

ones		tenths	hundredths
0	.	7	

ones		tenths	hundredths
0	.	1	9

Sometimes we can **simplify** a fraction to make it easier to work with. For example, the numerator and denominator of the fraction $\frac{14}{20}$ can both be divided by 2 ($14 \div 2 = 7$; $20 \div 2 = 10$). The simplified fraction is $\frac{7}{10}$.

There are two ways of changing a fraction to a decimal. One is to divide the numerator by the denominator. For example:

$$\frac{3}{20} = 3 \div 20 = 0.15$$

The second way is to multiply both the numerator and denominator by a number that makes the denominator equal 10, 100, or 1,000. For example:

$$\frac{3}{20} = \frac{3 \times 5}{20 \times 5} = \frac{15}{100} = 0.15$$

›GO FIGURE!

Use the figures below to find out what proportion of each shoal the sharks eat.

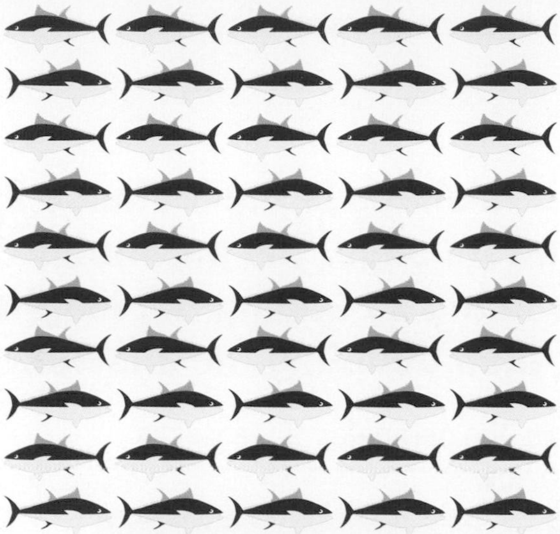

Shoal 1 has 50 tuna.

Shoal 2 has 100 sardines.

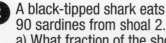

Shoal 3 has 144 herring.

1. A great white shark eats 15 tuna from shoal 1. a) What fraction of the shoal of tuna is this? Simplify your fraction, if you can. b) What is this proportion as a decimal?

2. A black-tipped shark eats 90 sardines from shoal 2. a) What fraction of the shoal of sardines is this? Simplify your fraction, if you can. b) What is this proportion as a decimal?

3. A silvertip reef shark eats 36 herring from shoal 3. a) What fraction of the shoal of herring is this? Simplify your fraction, if you can. b) What is this proportion as a decimal?

MISSION 8

SUNKEN RUINS

The remains of Cleopatra's palace and the lighthouse at Alexandria were found submerged beneath the Mediterranean Sea in Egypt. The Egyptian government wants to build an underwater museum. Your mission is to calculate the dimensions of these underwater ruins.

LEARN ABOUT IT
AREA AND PERIMETER

The perimeter **of a shape is the distance all the way around its edge. The perimeter of a** rectangle **is found by adding the length to the width, then doubling the answer.**

For example, the perimeter of the yellow rectangle below is:

(2 cm + 6 cm) × 2 = 16 cm

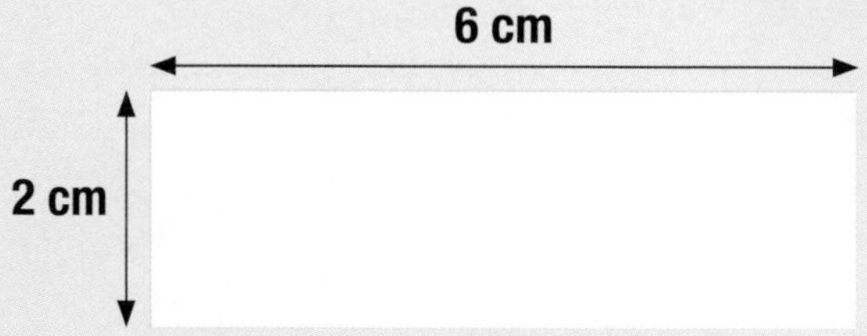

The area of a shape is the amount of surface inside it. The area of a rectangle is found by multiplying its length by its width. The answer is written in squared units. For the yellow rectangle, its area is:

$2 \times 6 = 12$ cm^2

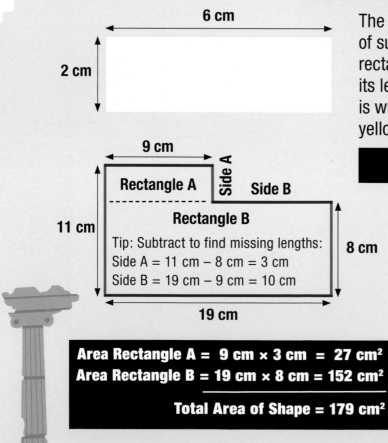

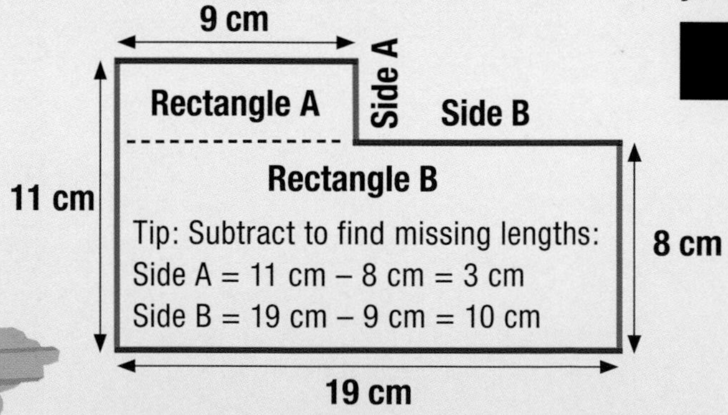

Area Rectangle A = 9 cm × 3 cm = 27 cm^2
Area Rectangle B = 19 cm × 8 cm = 152 cm^2

Total Area of Shape = 179 cm^2

When finding the area of a shape with squared corners and more than four straight sides, it is helpful to first try to split up the shape into rectangles. The dotted line in the shape to the left separates two rectangles. Then find the area of each rectangle separately and add them together.

›GO FIGURE!

You have used underwater equipment to measure the sizes of the city's ruined buildings and have sketched some of them on this chart. Use your knowledge of area and perimeter to gather more information on the sizes of the ruins.

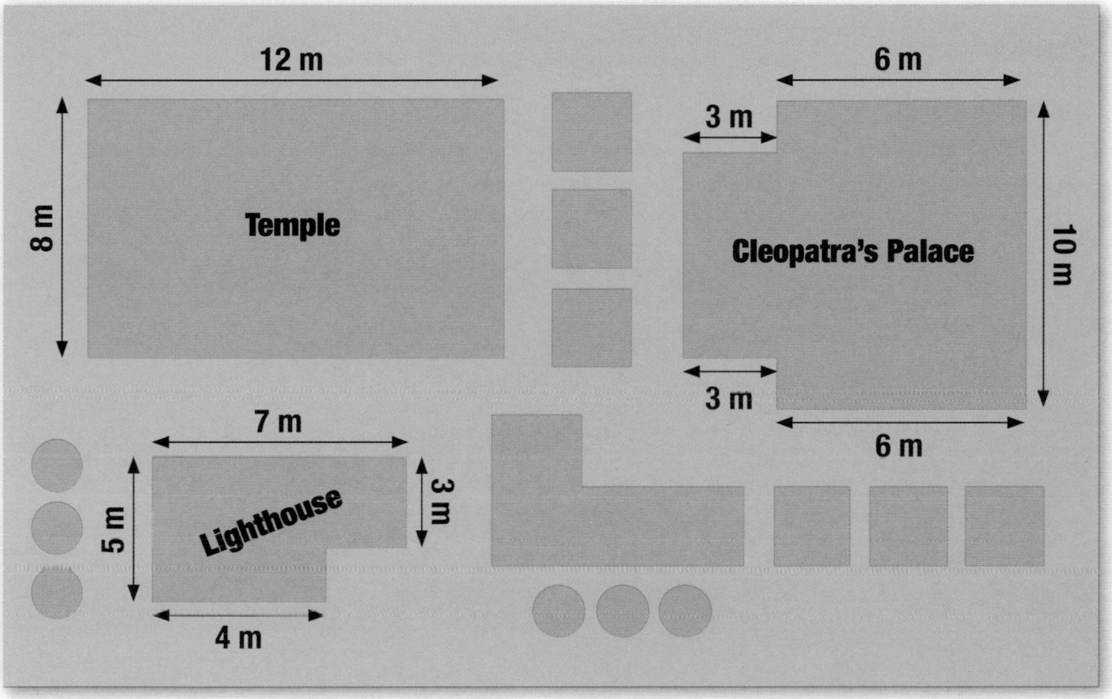

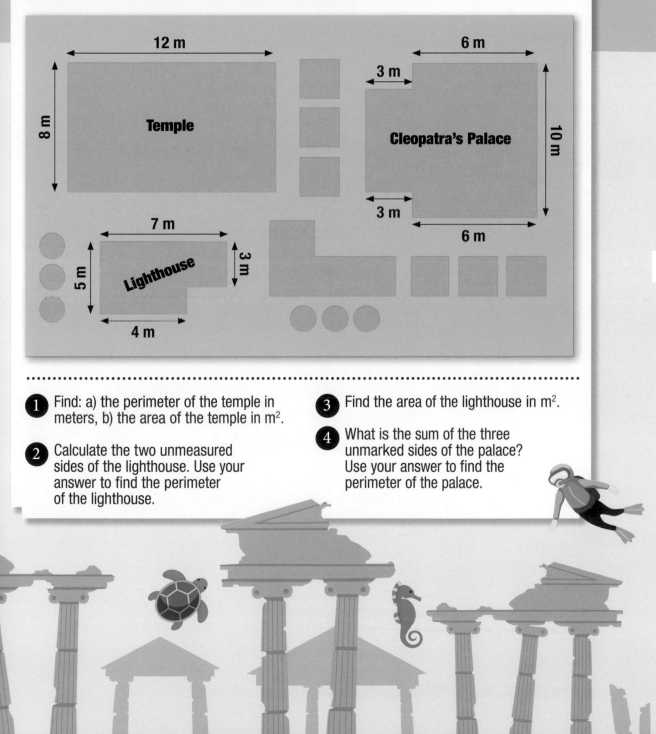

1. Find: a) the perimeter of the temple in meters, b) the area of the temple in m^2.
2. Calculate the two unmeasured sides of the lighthouse. Use your answer to find the perimeter of the lighthouse.
3. Find the area of the lighthouse in m^2.
4. What is the sum of the three unmarked sides of the palace? Use your answer to find the perimeter of the palace.

MISSION 9

WHALES

Next, you'll have a close encounter with a humpback whale, one of the largest animals on Earth. It is migrating on its annual journey from the North Pole to the equator, where it will give birth. Studying surface area to volume ratios will make it clear why the whales must migrate.

LEARN ABOUT IT

SURFACE AREA TO VOLUME RATIO

The surface area **of an object is the amount of surface it has. The** volume **is the amount of space the object takes up.**

For example, cube A has 6 faces, or individual surfaces. The area of each face is 1 square centimeter, or 1 cm^2. To find the surface area of the entire cube, add the area of all the faces together. So, cube A's surface area is:

$$1\ cm^2 + 1\ cm^2 + 1\ cm^2 + 1\ cm^2 + 1\ cm^2 + 1\ cm^2 = 6\ cm^2$$

OR $$6 \times 1\ cm^2 = 6\ cm^2$$

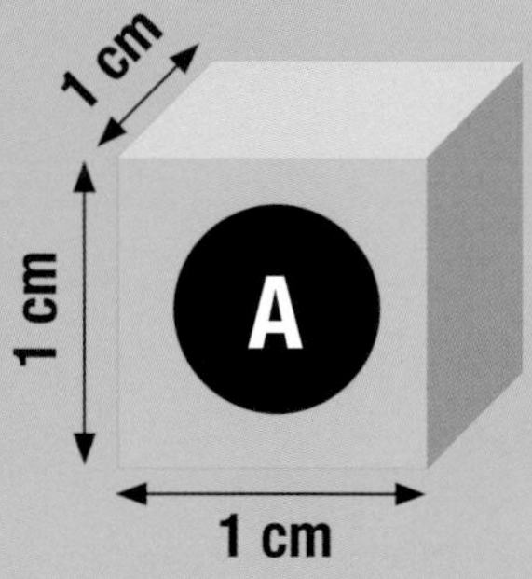

The volume of a cube is found by multiplying the length by the width by the height. Volume is measured in units cubed, such as cm^3.

$$V = l \times w \times h$$

So, the volume of cube A is $1\ cm \times 1\ cm \times 1\ cm = 1\ cm^3$.

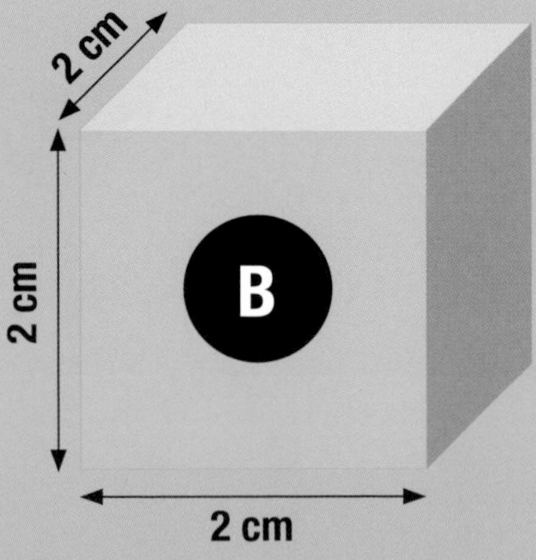

We compare the size of the surface area to the volume by writing it as a **ratio**. The surface area to volume ratio for cube A is 6:1. That means there is 6 times more surface area than volume in the cube.

In cube B, each of its 6 faces is 4 cm^2, so its surface area is 24 cm^2. Cube B's volume is $2\ cm \times 2\ cm \times 2\ cm = 8\ cm^3$, so its surface area to volume ratio is 24:8.

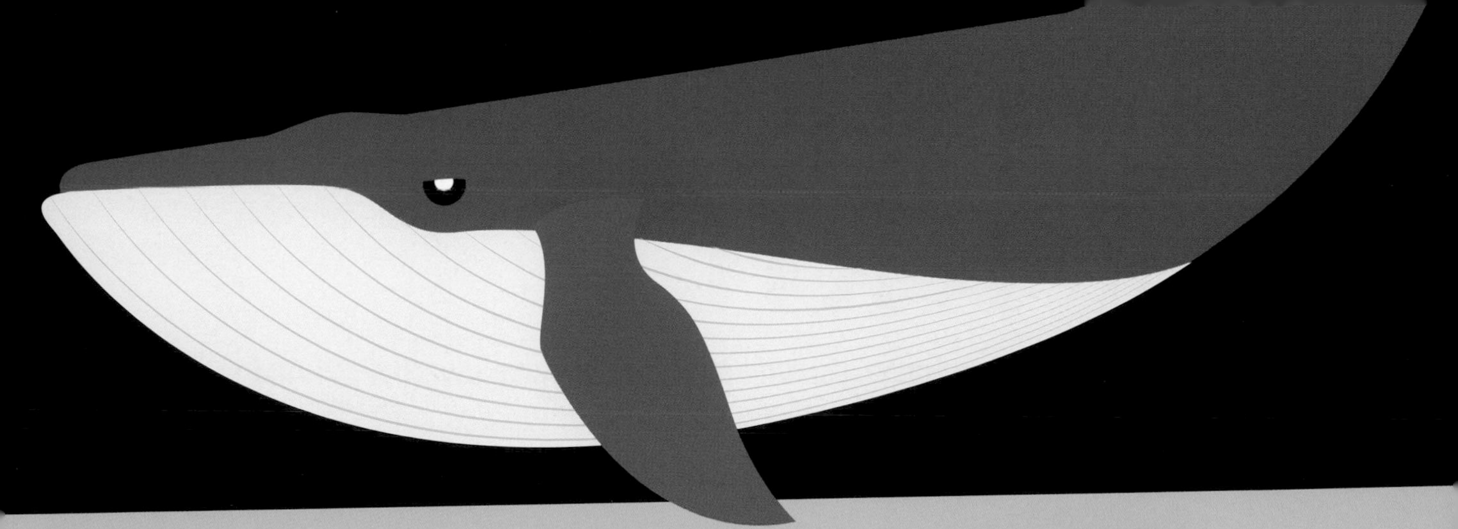

Like fractions, we can simplify ratios by dividing both numbers by the same number. Each number in the ratio 24:8 can be divided by 8. The simplifed ratio is the ratio 3:1.

›GO FIGURE!

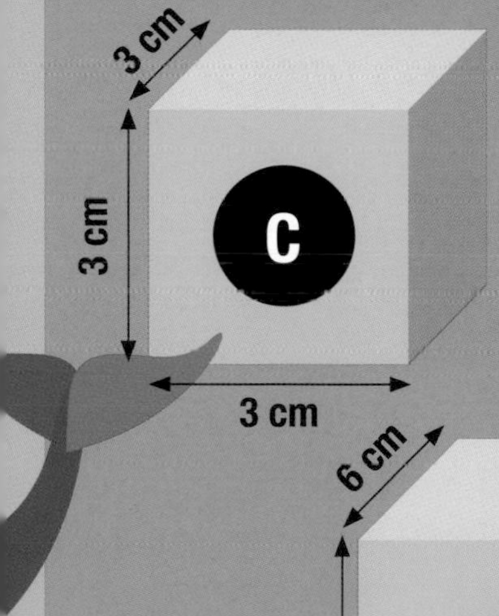

Large adult whales can survive in cold waters for a long time, but smaller baby whales cannot. That is why whales migrate to warmer waters to give birth. To get a better understanding, explore the surface area to volume ratio for smaller and larger objects.

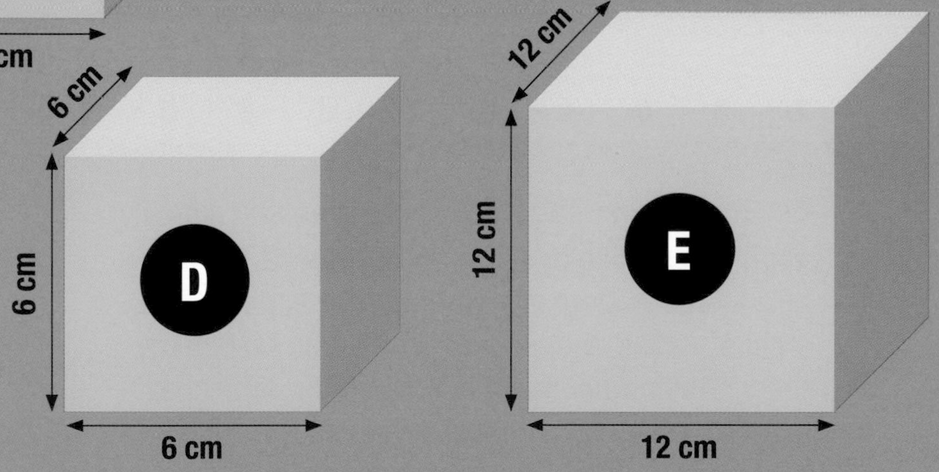

1. For each of the cubes C, D, and E, find the surface area to volume ratio, simplifying them to the form _ : 1, or 1: _ .
2. Which of the five cubes (A to E) on these pages has: a) the ratio of 1:1, b) the largest surface area to volume ratio, c) the ratio of 1:2?
3. As a cube gets smaller, does the surface area to volume ratio get bigger or smaller?
4. Whales lose heat through their body surface. Why do you think baby whales get colder quicker than adults?

MISSION 10

BILLIONS OF KRILL

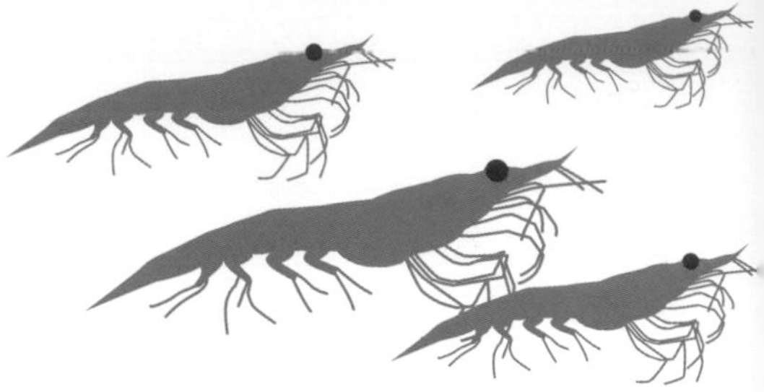

As you follow the whales, you will observe massive swarms of krill in the ocean. Krill are small, shrimp-like animals that whales eat by the **billions**. Your mission is to use your knowledge of large numbers to count the krill.

LEARN ABOUT IT
LARGE NUMBERS AND EXPONENTS

When describing large numbers, we group digits in threes from right to left. Groups of three are usually separated by a comma, as in this example: 51,000,000.

Billions			Millions			Thousands			Ones			
HB	TB	B	HM	TM	M	HTh	TTh	Th	H	T	O	
				5	1	0	0	0	0	0	0	fifty-one million
		2	3	0	0	0	0	0	0	0	0	two billion, three hundred million

O	Ones
T	Tens
H	Hundreds
Th	Thousands
TTh	Ten thousands
HTh	Hundred thousands
M	Millions
TM	Ten millions
HM	Hundred millions
B	Billions
TB	Ten billions
HB	Hundred billions

When a number has a lot of zeros, we can simplify what it looks like by using an **exponent**, or power, of 10. An exponent is a number that appears as a smaller raised number, and it tells you how many times the number on its left should be multiplied by itself. When 10 is multiplied together many times, we can write them using an exponent, like this:

$$10{,}000 = 10 \times 10 \times 10 \times 10 = 10^4$$

$$1{,}000{,}000 = 10 \times 10 \times 10 \times 10 \times 10 \times 10 = 10^6$$

The column headings below have been changed to show exponents:

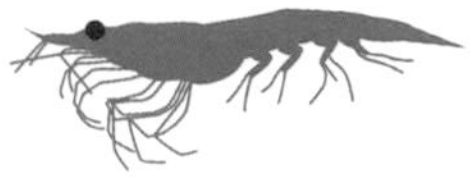

Billions			Millions			Thousands			Ones		
10^{11}	10^{10}	10^9	10^8	10^7	10^6	10^5	10^4	10^3	10^2	10	1
				5	1	0	0	0	0	0	0
		2	3	0	0	0	0	0	0	0	0

This number can be written as 5.1×10^7

This number can be written as 2.3×10^9

›GO FIGURE!

As you try to count the impossibly huge number of krill in the ocean, you'll need to know how to write very large numbers without using lots of digits. Krill are just 5 cm in length, but there are so many of them in our oceans that they form a huge part of the global food chain.

Recent estimates:

Number of people on the planet:	**7,000,000,000**
Mass (in kg) of all the Atlantic krill around Antarctica:	**900,000,000,000**
Mass (in kg) of krill born each year:	**490,000,000,000**
Total number of individual krill in the world:	**800,000,000,000,000**
Area (in km²) where krill are found in the summer:	**19,000,000**

1. Write in digits which of the numbers above is:
   a) nineteen million
   b) nine hundred billion
   c) eight hundred **trillion**

2. How many billions of kilograms of krill are born each year?

3. Write the estimated area (in km²) where krill are found in the summer using an exponent.

4. Write the estimated number of people on the planet:
   a) in words,
   b) using an exponent.

5. What is the total number of krill in the world, when using an exponent?

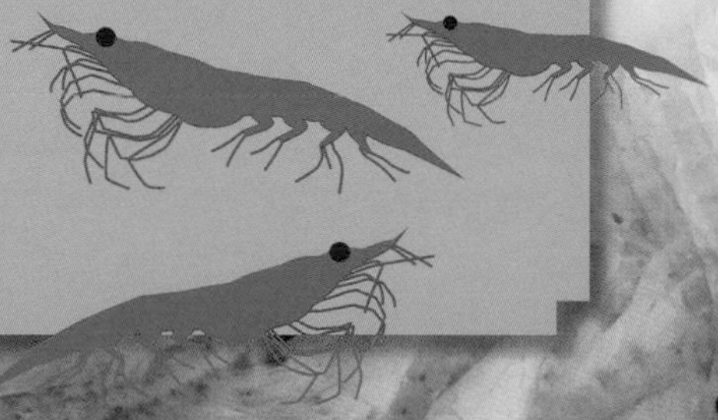

MISSION 11

UNDERWATER VOLCANO

Your next mission is your most dangerous yet—to measure the size of Kilauea, a volcano in Hawaii that grew from undersea eruptions. Molten lava is erupting from Kilauea all the time and super-heating the water around it.

LEARN ABOUT IT
CIRCLES AND CONES

First you need to learn about a special number, called pi, **which we use to figure out the** circumference, diameter, **area, and volume of circles and cones.**

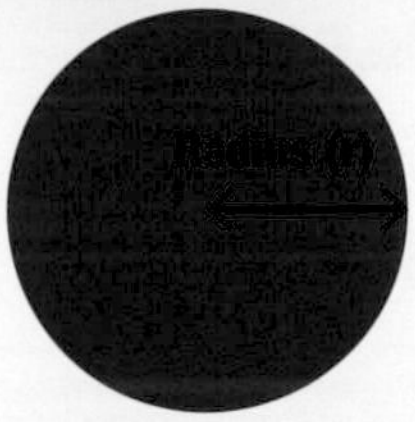

The **radius** of a circle is the distance from the edge to the center of the circle.

The diameter is the widest distance across the circle, through the center.

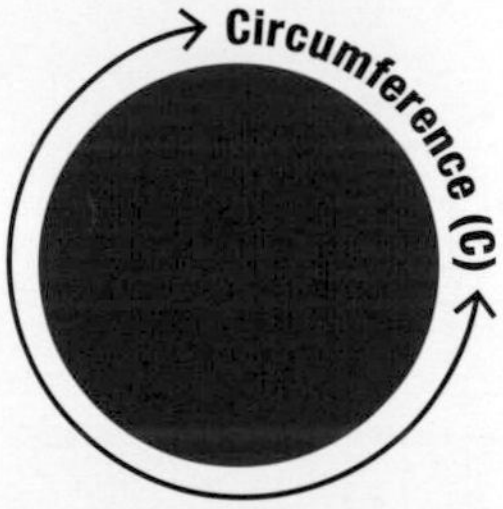

The circumference is another word for the perimeter of the circle.

There is a special relationship between the diameter (d) of a circle and its circumference (C). For every circle, the circumference will always be 3.1412… times the diameter. (The … means the number goes on longer than is shown here.) We call this number pi. The mathematical symbol for pi is π. Pi is a never-ending number, so it is usually rounded to 3.14 when calculating formulas.

The formula for circumference can be written as $C = \pi \times d$. Note: Formulas are often written without the multiplication signs.

$$C = \pi d$$

or

$$C = 2\pi r$$

Because the radius is half the diameter, the formula can also be written as $C = \pi \times 2 \times r$.

To find the area of a circle, use the formula Area = $\pi \times \text{radius}^2$. (When you multiply something by itself, we say it is squared (^{2}). Squaring is performed first.) The short form of the formula can also be written as:

$$A = \pi r^2$$

The formula for the volume (V) of a **cone** using the radius (r) and the height (h) is $V = \frac{1}{3} \times \pi \times r \times r \times h$. The short form of the formula can also be written as:

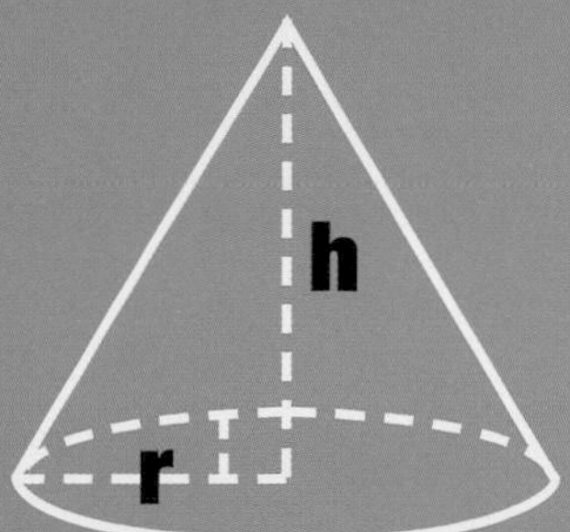

$$V = \frac{1}{3}\pi r^2 h$$

GO FIGURE!

You travel around the edge of the cone-shaped volcano and estimate that its diameter at the base under water is approximately 6 km. You estimate that its height is about 700 m.

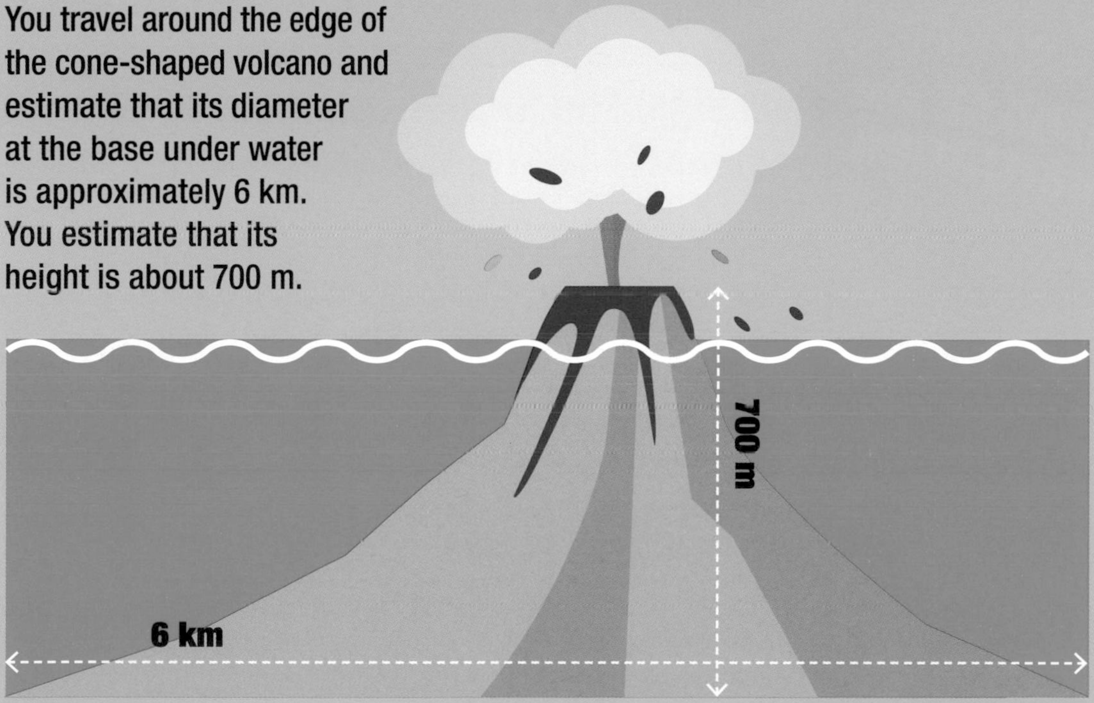

1. What is the approximate radius of the volcano?
2. Taking π to be 3.14, find the approximate circumference of the volcano at its base, to the nearest km.
3. Using your answer to question 1, find the approximate area of the circular base of the volcano.
4. What is the height of the volcano in km? (Hint: There are 1,000 meters in a kilometer.)
5. Using the formula on this page, find the approximate volume of the volcano in km^3. Round your answer to 1 decimal point.
6. One of the largest volcanoes in the world is Piton de la Fournaise on Réunion Island. The diameter at its base is 220 km, and it is about 6 km tall. What is its approximate volume in km^3?

MISSION 12

DON'T GET THE BENDS

Your final mission is to return to the surface safely! The changes in pressure that take place when you rise to the surface can be very dangerous if you go too quickly. Divers always rise slowly so they don't get a sickness called the bends.

LEARN ABOUT IT

FORMULAE AND SUBSTITUTION

Algebra is a branch of math that uses formulas to show relationships between things. The formulas use letters or symbols to stand in for different things.

There's a formula that will help you calculate the time you must take to rise to the surface of the ocean safely without getting the bends.

The formula that shows the relationship between the number of seconds, N, you must take to rise safely through a given depth, D, in meters is $N = 6 \times D$. We can substitute a number into the formula to find the other value.

N = 6D

So, rising safely from a depth of 110 m below sea level takes $N = 6 \times 110 = 660$ seconds.

N = 6 × 110 = 660 seconds

This time can then be converted into minutes and seconds.

660 seconds = 11 minutes

Remember:
1 minute = 60 seconds
2 minutes = 120 seconds
3 minutes = 180 seconds

How quickly can you rise safely from a depth of 0.2 km below sea level?

N = 6 × 200 = 1,200 seconds = 20 minutes

Remember:
1 kilometer
= 1,000 meters

›GO FIGURE!

Calculate the appropriate amount of time you would need to safely rise from different depths using the formula and making substitutions in the data given.

1. How many seconds, N, should you take to rise from a depth, D, of:
a) 9 m, b) 40 m,
c) 0.3 km, d) 0.5 km,
e) 600 m?

2. Write the answers for b, c, d, and e in question 1 in minutes.

3. A fellow diver tells you she will rise from a depth of 400 m in 40 minutes. Is this safe?

4. If you take 24 seconds to rise to the surface, what is the maximum safe depth you should have started from?

5. If you take 20 minutes and 12 seconds to rise to the surface, what is the maximum safe depth you should have started from?

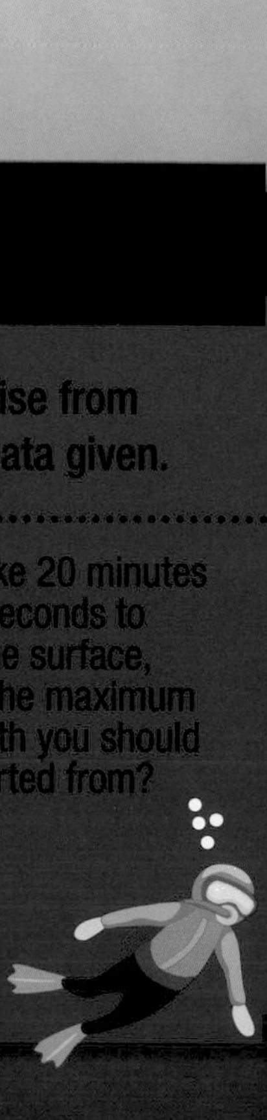

GO FIGURE! ANSWERS

04–05 Learning to dive

1. a) -40 is the deepest.
b) -6, -18, -25, -32, -40
2. a) -35 + 10 = -25 m
b) -25 – 17 = -42 m
3. 28 – 7 = 21 m
4. a) 31 – 3 = 28 m, b) 31 – 16 = 15 m
c) 31 + 2 = 33 m

06–07 Coral reefs

1. a) 250 – 200 = 50 km^2
b) 320 – 224 = 96 km^2
c) 900 – 495 = 405 km^2
2. They have all decreased in size.
3. Reef A: $\frac{50}{250} \times 100 = 20\%$
Reef B: $\frac{96}{320} \times 100 = 30\%$
Reef C: $\frac{405}{900} \times 100 = 45\%$
4. Reef C's area has had the greatest percentage change.
5. 400,000 - 280,000 = 120,000 difference.
So the percentage change is:

$$\frac{120,000}{400,000} \times 100 = 30\%$$

08–09 Shipwreck

1. a) (-4,5) b) (-5,-3)
c) (2,-5) d) (4,0)
2. a) Treasure chest
b) Musket (pistol)
3. (4,2) (5,2) (6,2)
4. 8 squares left and 7 squares down
5. a) Treasure chest b) Cannon

10–11 Ocean bed

1. 1) -4400 m 2) -4000 m 3) -5800 m
4) -6000 m 5) -7400 m 6) -8200 m
7) -8000 m 8) -6400 m
2. a) 8200 – 4000 = 4,200 m
b) 8000 – 6000 = 2,000 m
3. -4400 – 4000 – 5800 – 6000 – 7400 – 8200 – 8000 – 6400 = -50,200 ÷ 8 = -6275 m
4. Reading 8 is the most representative.

12–13 Submarines

1. a) 30 kph, b) -500 m, -3000 m, -5500 m
2. a) 80 psi b) 30 psi
3. 247,615 – 247,395 = 220 nautical miles
4. 12 – 7 = 5 hours
220 ÷ 5 = 44 knots average speed

14–15 Watch out!

1. a) (5,3) b) (3,1) c) (-2,-4) d) (-4,-6)
2. No
3. y = x – 4
4. (4,8) (1,2) (0,0) and (-1,-2)

16–17 Shoals and sharks

1. a) $\frac{15}{50}$ or $\frac{3}{10}$ b) $\frac{3}{10}$ = 0.3
2. a) $\frac{90}{100}$ or $\frac{9}{10}$ b) $\frac{9}{10}$ = 0.9
3. a) $\frac{36}{144}$ or $\frac{9}{36}$ or $\frac{1}{4}$ b) $\frac{1}{4}$ = 0.25

18–19 Sunken ruins

1. a) $(12 + 8) \times 2 = 40$ m b) $12 \times 8 = 96$ m^2
2. Side A: 5 m – 3 m = 2 m
   Side B: 7 m – 4m = 3 m
   Perimeter is $7 + 5 + 4 + 2 + 3 + 3 = 24$ m
3. $(5 \times 4) + (3 \times 3) = 20 + 9 = 29$ m^2 or
   $(7 \times 3) + (4 \times 2) = 21 + 8 = 29$ m^2
4. The three unmarked sides add up to 10 m (to match the length of the opposite side).
   Perimeter is $10 + 3 + 3 + 6 + 10 + 6 = 38$ m

20–21 Whales

1. C) Surface area is 6×9 cm^2 = 54 cm^2
   Volume is $3 \times 3 \times 3 = 27$ cm^3,
   so ratio is 2:1
   D) Surface area is 6×36 cm^2 = 216 cm^2
   Volume is $6 \times 6 \times 6 = 216$ cm^3,
   so ratio is 1:1
   E) Surface area is 6×144 cm^2 = 864 cm^2
   Volume is $12 \times 12 \times 12 = 1728$ cm^3,
   so ratio is 1:2
2. a) D, b) A, c) E
3. Bigger.
4. The larger the surface area is in relation to the volume, the more surface they have to lose their body heat through. Larger adults have proportionally more inner space and less surface area, so they lose their body heat more slowly.

22–23 Billions of krill

1. a) 19,000,000
   b) 900,000,000,000
   c) 800,000,000,000,000
2. 490 billion
3. $19{,}000{,}000 = 1.9 \times 10^7$
4. a) Seven billion
   b) 7×10^9 or 7.0×10^9
5. 8×10^{14} or 8.0×10^{14}

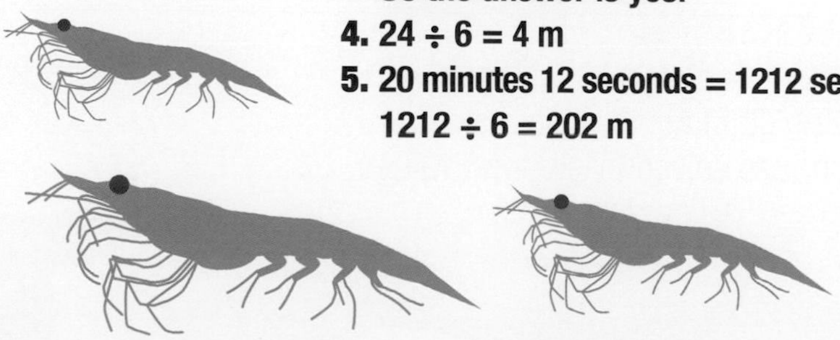

24–25 Underwater volcano

1. $6 \div 2 = 3$ km radius
2. 6×3.14 = approximately 19 km circumference
3. $(3 \times 3) \times 3.14$ = approximately 28 km^2 area of the base
4. 700 m = 0.7 km
5. $\frac{1}{3} \times 3.14 \times (3 \times 3) \times 0.7$ = approximately 6.6 km^3 volume of cone
6. $\frac{1}{3} \times 3.14 \times (110 \times 110) \times 6$ = approximately 75,988 km^3 volume of cone

26–27 Don't get the bends

1. a) $9 \times 6 = 54$ seconds
   b) $40 \times 6 = 240$ seconds
   c) 0.3 km = 300 m,
   so $300 \times 6 = 1800$ seconds
   d) 0.5 km = 500 m,
   so $500 \times 6 = 3000$ seconds
   e) $600 \times 6 = 3600$ seconds
2. $240 \div 60 = 4$ minutes
   $1800 \div 60 = 30$ minutes
   $3000 \div 60 = 50$ minutes
   $3600 \div 60 = 60$ minutes
3. $400 \times 6 = 2400$ seconds
   $2400 \div 60 = 40$ minutes
   So the answer is yes.
4. $24 \div 6 = 4$ m
5. 20 minutes 12 seconds = 1212 seconds
   $1212 \div 6 = 202$ m

MATH GLOSSARY

AREA
The amount of two-dimensional space covered by a shape or an object. For example, the area of a rectangle is calculated by multiplying the length of one of the short sides by the length of one of the long sides.

BILLION
A thousand million

CIRCUMFERENCE
The perimeter of a circle, which is the distance all the way around the edge

CONE
A solid shape with a circular base and one point, or vertex

COORDINATES
A series of numbers that will locate a point on a grid with two axes

DATA
A collection of facts or information

DIAMETER
The widest length across a circle, passing through the center

EQUATION
A statement that says two things on either side of an equals sign are equal. Equations are solved by entering values.

EXPONENT
A small raised number to the right of another number, that says how many times to multipy that number by itself. Also called a power, the number is written in the form 10^6.

FORMULA
An equation that shows the relationship between two different quantities

KNOT
A speed traveling on water that is equivalent to 1 nautical mile per hour

LINEAR GRAPH
A graph that shows the relationship in which the amount goes up or down in the same amount each time, forming a straight line. It is sometimes called a straight-line graph.

MEAN AVERAGE
A number found by adding all the values in a set of data and dividing by the number of values there are

NAUTICAL
Relating to navigation at sea or ships

NEGATIVE NUMBER
A number that is less than zero. We write negative numbers using the minus sign (-), e.g. -5, -3, -7.

PERCENTAGE
A fraction with a denominator of 100

PERIMETER
The total distance around a two-dimensional shape

PI
The relationship between the diameter and circumference of a circle. It is written as π, and equal to roughly 3.14.

POSITIVE NUMBER
A number that is greater than zero

QUADRANT
One of the four sections created when a shape is divided by two lines that cross, such as the x-axis and y-axis

RECTANGLE
A four-sided shape in which all four corners have an angle of 90°

RADIUS
The distance between the center of a circle and its edge

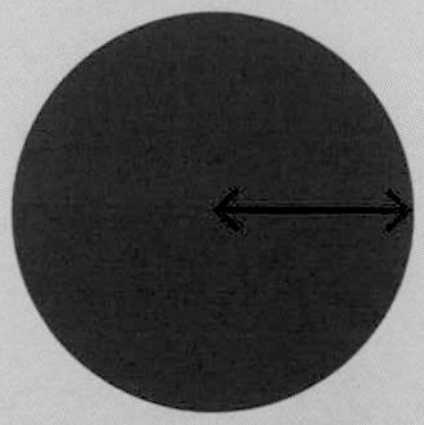

RATIO
A way to show how a number or value is related to another. A ratio of 2:1 shows that there are twice as many of the first value as there are of the second.

SIMPLIFY/SIMPLEST FORM
To simplify a fraction, we change it to an equivalent fraction that uses smaller numbers, e.g. $\frac{6}{8} = \frac{3}{4}$. When a number cannot be simplified, it is in its simplest form. Ratios can also be simplified in the same way: 4:12 = 1:3.

SURFACE AREA
The amount of two-dimensional space covered by the surface of an object. It is found by adding up the areas of all the object's sides.

TRILLION
A thousand billion

VALUE
The total amount that a number or group of numbers adds up to

VOLUME
The amount of space an object takes up. It is measured in cubic units, such as cubic centimeters (cm^3) or cubic meters (m^3).

LEARNING MORE

WEBSITES

www.mathisfun.com
A huge website packed full of explanations, examples, games, puzzles, activities, worksheets, and teacher resources for all age levels.

www.khanacademy.org
A learning resource website for all ages, it contains practice exercises and easy-to-follow instructional videos on all subjects, including math.

www.mathplayground.com
An action-packed website with math games, mathematical word problems, worksheets, puzzles, and videos.

INDEX